Dedicated to my three
amazing grandchildren.

ISBN: 978-0-9852587-4-0 (hardcover)
ISBN: 978-0-9852587-3-3 (paperback)
ISBN: 978-0-9852587-5-7 (ebook)

Written by Diane Trusilo LaFrance

Illustrated by Ekaterina Ilchenko

Published by Delightful Bee

April 25, 2026

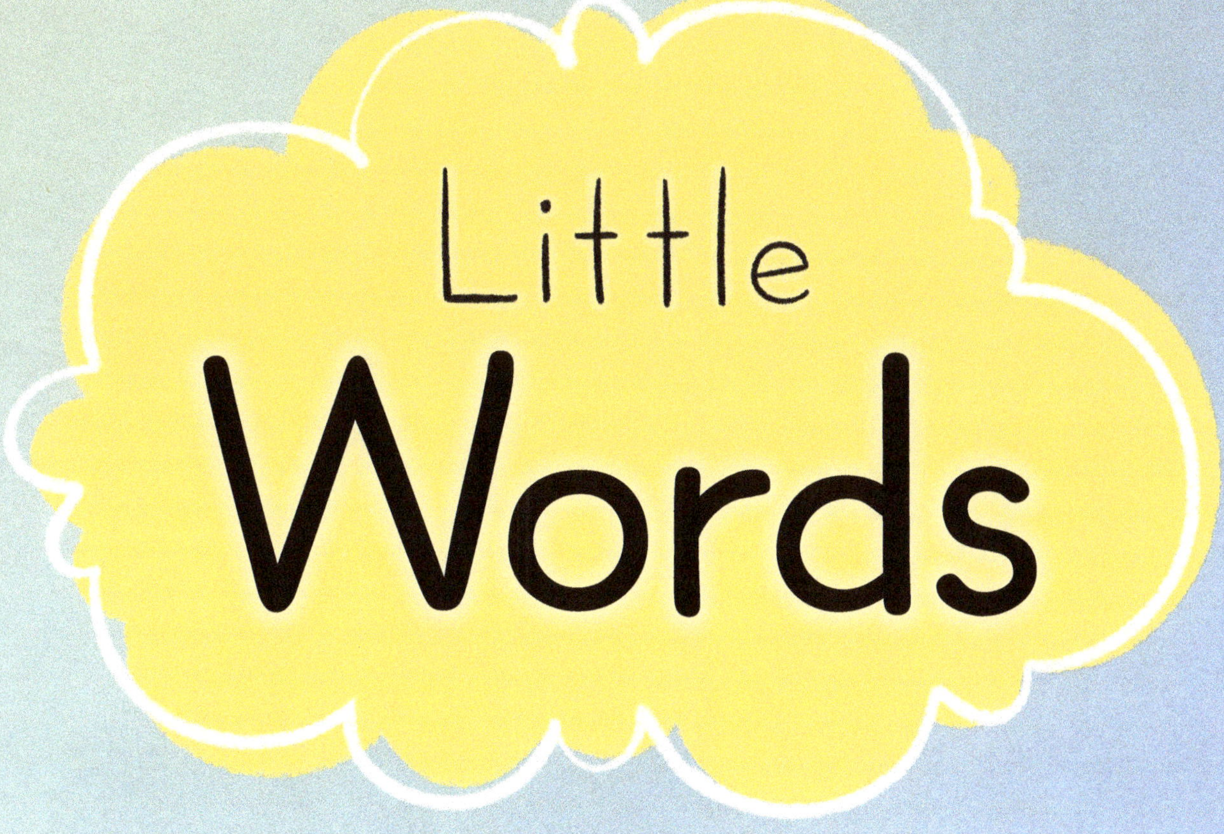

Little Words

Diane Trusilo LaFrance

Ekaterina Ilchenko

The Little Word Parade

The little words are coming
The little words are coming
One by one
Here they come
Looking for some fun
Each one beating to its very own drum
The little words are coming
One by one
Here they come

if it is in
it is not out

If it is in
It is not out
The little words are coming
The little words are coming
One by one
Here they come

Here and There

The words went up
The words went down
They went up
They went down
They went up and down
And all around the town
The words went here
The words went there
They went everywhere they wanted to go
And then they went back home

is
at
me
that

Words Like to Play

Words like to play with you
They like to hide up in the tree
If you look
You will see

be we see she
three he and me

Hiding up in the big old tree
Try to find them and when you do
You will feel so proud of you

three
he
she
me
be
see
we

A Little Word

So many little words for you and me
So many words for our eyes to see
Here there and everywhere
Some little words rhyme
All little words are one of a kind
Just like you and me

are
they
it
said
is
me

It is Fun to Be With You

It is fun to be with you
There are so many things we can do
We can ride a bike or take a hike
We can take a walk or just sit and talk
What do you want to do today
Do you want to bake a cake
Or go for a swim in the lake
Do you want to go out to play
Or just stay inside all day
What do you want to do
It is always fun to be with you
No matter what we do

One Two Three Four

1 2 3 4
One two three four
Words are walking out the door

have has had one

Learning words can be fun

this

that

then

they

Words are going out to play

two
four
three
2
2
4
4
3
3

Funny Little Words

Some words can be funny like
  you and me
Some words can be tricky like
  have and of
Some words are opposites like
  up and down
  over and under
  big and little
  old and new
Some words are rhyming words like
  come and some
  walk and talk
  my by why and I
  so no and go
So many words we must know
  is and his
  as and has
  me he we she be and see
  good could should and would
And then we have said and red
They like to read in bed

said red

We Are the Words

We are the words

The **mighty mighty** words
We are here for you
We can help you
You will see
All you have to do is

Read

read

read

You can read this
You can read that
You can read to a cat

Up and Away

The words go up and down
In and out
Here and there
All without a care

Some words are big and some are little
Some words like to make us giggle

Words like to play with you
They like to play games too

Me he we see she and be
Are hiding in the big old tree

So no and go
are playing in the snow

Why my by and I
are floating across the sky

I
why
my

What Do You Want to Do

What kinds of things do you like to do
What makes you happy being you
Do you like to ride a bike
Do you like to take a hike
Do you like to play outside
Do you like to run and hide
What kinds of things do you like to do
Do you like to read a book
Sitting by a little brook
So many things for you to do
What kinds of things do you like to do

So Many Words

If it is little
It is not big
If it is in
It is not out
Big and little
In and out
These are the words we are talking about

If it is up
It is not down
Big and little
Up and down
In and out
These are the words we are talking about

Come and some
Walk and talk
We can write words with chalk

We can look here
We can look there
We can find words everywhere

We can find words in a book
We can find words on a box
We can find words on rocks

We can look here
We can look there
Words are EVERYWHERE

Big words

Big words
Little words
Words words words

Words can do so many things
Words can make you feel happy
Words can make you feel sad

Words can tell you what to do
Words can help when you're feeling blue
Words can take you to places you know
    and to places you want to go
Words can tell you things like
Who what when where why

Who went there
What did they do
When did they go
Where did they go
Why did they go
Who what when where why

Big words
Little words
Words words words

About the Author

When I was little, I remember wondering how I would ever learn to read all the words in books. Years later, as a first-grade teacher, I had the joy of helping children discover that they could do exactly that. After many years in the classroom, I wrote this book to make learning sight words a little more meaningful, engaging, and fun for beginning readers.

I am so grateful to Ekaterina Ilchenko for her incredible artistic talent and bringing life to all the Little Words in the book.

About the Illustrator

While working on this book, I imagined the little words coming to life and playing together. It was a pleasure to illustrate Diane LaFrance's poems and bring these playful characters into the world of Little Words.

www.ingramcontent.com/pod-product-compliance
Lightning Source LLC
Chambersburg PA
CBHW040905070726
47599CB00038B/2310